D1538896

THE NORTHERN COLONIES:
Freedom to Worship (1600-1770)

TITLE LIST

THE NORTHERN COLONIES:
Freedom to Worship (1600-1770)

BY TERESA LACLAIR

MASON CREST

Mason Crest
370 Reed Road
Broomall, Pennsylvania 19008
www.masoncrest.com

Printed and bound in Hashemite Kingdom of Jordan.

First printing
9 8 7 6 5 4 3 2 1

Library of Congress Cataloging-in-Publication Data

LaClair, Teresa.
  The northern colonies : freedom to worship (1600-1770) / by Teresa LaClair.
    p. cm. — (How America became America)
  Includes bibliographical references and index.
  ISBN 978-1-4222-2397-0 (hardcover) — ISBN 978-1-4222-2396-3 (hard cover series) ISBN 978-1-4222-9307-2 (ebook)
  1. Freedom of religion—Northeastern States—History—17th century—Juvenile literature. 2. Freedom of religion—Northeastern States—History—18th century—Juvenile literature. 3. Freedom of religion—United States—History—17th century—Juvenile literature. 4. Freedom of religion—United States—History—18th century—Juvenile literature. 5. United States—History—Colonial period, ca. 1600-1775—Juvenile literature. I. Title.
  BR516.L244 2012
  261.7'20974—dc22
                          2011000838

Produced by Harding House Publishing Services, Inc.
www.hardinghousepages.com
Cover design by Torque Advertising + Design.

1603—James I becomes king.

Spring 1608—A group of Separatists flees to the Netherlands, because they aren't allowed to practice their religion in England.

1623—The Dutch create New Netherland and build Fort Orange near what is Albany, New York, today.

1625—Charles I becomes king.

October 1635—Roger Williams is sent away from the Massachusetts Bay Colony because of his strong beliefs. He travels to Rhode Island and starts the city of Providence with a few friends and family members.

September 1609—Henry Hudson finds the Hudson River while looking for the Northwest Passage.

1626—Peter Minuit buys the island of Manhattan from the Native Americans for the Dutch.

June 1636—Thomas Hooker and a group of one hundred people leave Massachusetts Bay and start the colony of Connecticut. The first city they build is called Hartford.

Autumn 1620—The Separatists leave the Netherlands and travel to North America on the Mayflower.

Early Summer 1630—The Winthrop Fleet, a group of seven hundred Puritans on eleven ships, starts the Massachusetts Bay Colony.

April 24, 1638—John Davenport creates New Haven, Connecticut, a separate colony from Hartford.

1647—Peter Stuyvesant becomes governor of New Netherland.

August 27, 1664—The English Duke of York attacks New Amsterdam. He wins, and in September gives control of New Netherland to the English.

1638—Anne Hutchinson is sent away from Massachusetts Bay for her beliefs. She is never allowed to return.

1649—In England, Parliament arrests King Charles I and has him beheaded. Instead of a king, Parliament rules England for the next eleven years.

1664—The New Haven colony joins the rest of the Connecticut colony.

January 14, 1639—Three Connecticut towns approve the Fundamental Orders. They all agree to obey some of the same rules, making them the Commonwealth of Connecticut.

Summer 1655—Led by Peter Stuyvesant, the Dutch capture New Sweden.

1681—William Penn purchases part of New Jersey and gets another piece of land from King Charles II. He names the colony Pennsylvania after his father.

1660—Charles II becomes king of England.

March 1638—The Swedish build Fort Christina in what is today Wilmington, Delaware.

The *Mayflower*

Chapter One
PLYMOUTH COLONY

Everyone was sick of sailing. Sixty-five long days had gone by since they had set out from England on September 6, 1620. The trip had been awful—cold and stormy. One storm had been so bad that water had leaked down through the deck. One of the ship's main beams had cracked. Many of the 102 passengers wondered if the *Mayflower* could really make it all the way across the ocean. But the ship's captain was sure the *Mayflower* could handle the journey. So on they went, sailing across the ocean to America.

Many of the passengers on the *Mayflower* were people called Separatists. They were part of a religious group known as the Puritans. The Church of England (the Anglican Church) had broken away from the Roman Catholic Church back in 1534. The Puritans thought leaving the Roman Catholic Church had been a good thing, but they thought the Anglicans hadn't made enough changes. Many Puritans thought they should stay a part of the Anglican Church. They wanted to help change the church while still being part of it. The Separatists, on the other hand, left the Anglican Church and started meeting on their own. This was against the law.

The Separatists wanted to worship God the way they wanted. They had tried moving to the Netherlands a few years earlier, but they had been unhappy there. They didn't know Dutch very well. They weren't able to grow food for themselves.

Meanwhile, the King of England had told the Virginia Company to build a **colony** called Virginia in the **New World**. The Separatists got permission from the Virginia Company to settle in America. This seemed like a pretty good answer to the Separatists' problems.

So now, after many setbacks, the Separatists were finally on their way to America. With them went a number of people who were just looking for adventure and a new life. Together, they became known as the Pilgrims.

Everyone was happy when they finally spotted land, but the ship's captain knew they were too far north.

"This is Cape Cod," he told them. "It's not even under the control of the Virginia Company."

But the weather was bad. The passengers really didn't want to go on. So the ship dropped anchor in what was later called Provincetown Harbor. Everyone went ashore. This was a better place for a colony anyway, people said to each other. Here, they wouldn't even have to worry about the Virginia Company telling them what to do.

A **colony** is a group of people living in a land outside of their original country. They still have to take orders from the government of their homeland.

European settlers called North and South America the **New World.** It was a new place for them, but a very old place for the people who had always lived there.

The Pilgrims depart from England

For the next month and a half, the Pilgrims looked around for a good place to build their colony. Finally, they decided on a spot across the bay, near an empty **Native** village. They called the new colony Plymouth, after the town they had sailed from in England.

By now it was late in December. The weather was freezing and snowy. Everyone agreed to first build one big building they could share. Then each man would work on his own house. Until then, everyone stayed on the *Mayflower*.

When the big building was finished, many of the Pilgrims moved into it. The building wasn't very big for over one hundred people, though. It was square, and each side was twenty feet long.

People had started getting sick not long after the Pilgrims arrived in the New World. They were cold and tired. The food wasn't very good. Some people died of a sickness called scurvy, caused by not having enough **vitamin C**. Others got sick with other diseases. More and more people died. By the time that first winter was over, half the Pilgrims had died. Half of the ship's crew had also died. Only seven people managed to stay healthy all winter.

In the spring, people started to feel better. They could spend time outside now, instead of being packed inside with other sick people. They worked on their houses. They planted gardens and explored the land around their new colony.

Then, in the middle of March, a Native man suddenly walked into the little village. The Pilgrims were surprised and nervous. This wasn't the first Native person they had

A **Native** is someone who has lived in a place his whole life. It can also mean Native American.

Vitamin C is a vitamin that helps your body fight diseases.

Squanto's arrival

met. Not long after they had landed at the tip of Cape Cod, a group of Nauset Indians had shot arrows into the Pilgrims' camp. The Pilgrims had fired back at them with their rifles. Luckily, no one had been hurt.

This man seemed friendly, though. He knew a little English, and he told them his name was Samoset. He had come from further north along the coast (from what is now Maine). He left after talking with the men for a while. Then a week later he came back. This time, he brought several other men with him.

One of the new men was called Squanto. Together, Samoset and Squanto helped the Pilgrims make a peace **treaty** with Massasoit, the leader of the Wampanoags. The Wampanoags were the Native **tribe** that lived nearest to the Plymouth colony.

Without the help of Squanto, the Pilgrims would have had a tough time surviving the next few years. Squanto showed them how to live in their new home. He hunted with them. He told them which roots and berries were good to eat. He taught them to use fish as **fertilizer** when they planted corn. The fish made the new crop grow tall and healthy.

In the fall, the Pilgrims invited the Wampanoag to a feast to celebrate their first harvest. The tables were filled with food. The Pilgrims and the Wampanoag ran races and played games together. This was the first Thanksgiving celebration.

Myles Standish was almost as important as Squanto to the new colony. Standish was not one

Massasoit's treaty with the Pilgrims

A **treaty** is an agreement between two people or groups.

A **tribe** is a group of people that live together and share the same way of life.

Fertilizers can make crops grow faster, stronger, or both.

A **military** leader is someone who protects people using weapons and battle.

of the Separatists who had come to the New World looking for the religious freedom. Instead, he was a soldier. The Separatists had hired him to be their **military** captain.

Standish did a lot more than take care of military things, though. He had been one of the seven people who hadn't gotten sick during the first winter, so he had helped look after the others. Later, he became close friends with one of the Wampanoag Indians. Standish helped lead the Pilgrims' colony.

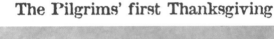

The Pilgrims' first Thanksgiving

THE MAYFLOWER COMPACT

Before the Pilgrims went ashore for the first time, they had some things to talk about. If they had landed where they were supposed to, they would have had to follow the laws of the Virginia Company. But here, there were no laws.

The Pilgrim men agreed they should govern themselves. All of them together would help to make the decisions about their new colony. They wrote up the Mayflower Compact and signed it. (The women were not allowed to take part in this.)

The Mayflower Compact was the beginning of the way Americans think about government. The idea that the people should rule themselves was part of America from the very beginning.

The signing of the Mayflower Compact

As the years went by, more people started to arrive from England. Plymouth grew, and new settlements sprang up.

Plymouth had become an important English colony.

Chapter Two
THE MASSACHUSETTS BAY COLONY

All through the summer of 1630, ships sailed into Massachusetts Bay.
The ships were filled with Puritan colonists, but they weren't headed
for Plymouth. Instead, they were going forty miles north of Plymouth.
They were going to the new colonies of Boston and Salem.

A few years before, King Charles I had agreed to let a group of Puritan businessmen
settle in the New World. They formed the Massachusetts Bay Company. They would
pay the king part of any money they made. Other than that, they could do what they
wanted.

Settlers started arriving at the new colonies. Life was hard for people there, so at first,
new settlers were slow to come.

But in England, a lot of Puritans were still unhappy in the Anglican Church. They
hadn't given up on changing things, but when Charles I had become king in 1625, he
made the Puritans nervous. His queen was a French Roman Catholic. The Puritans
worried that England would become more Catholic again. When a Catholic queen had
been in power last time, a lot of Puritans had been killed. What if that happened again?

The only control the Puritans had over the king was through **Parliament**. Parliament kept the king from having too much power. But then, in 1629, King Charles closed down Parliament. He was tired of Parliament trying to control him. Suddenly, lots of Puritans wanted to leave England.

In 1630, seventeen ships filled with Puritan families arrived in Massachusetts Bay. Eleven of them arrived together in a group called the Winthrop Fleet.

John Winthrop, the new **governor** of the Massachusetts Bay Colony, was excited about the new colony. He believed England and the rest

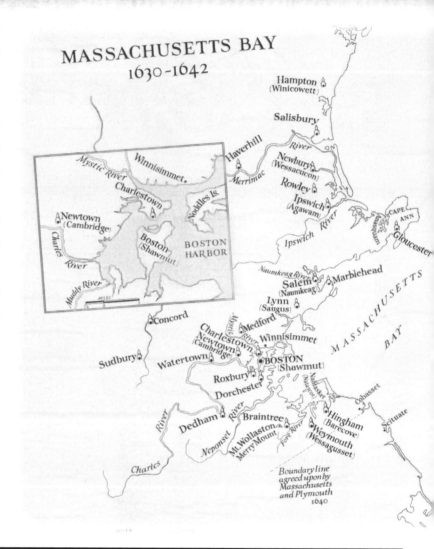

MASSACHUSETTS BAY
1630–1642

Parliament is a group of British leaders who make up one part of the government.

A **governor** is a leader of a state or territory.

of Europe had become completely evil. All good people should leave, he thought. God would punish Europe soon, and he didn't want to be there for that!

Winthrop had an idea about what the Massachusetts Bay Colony should be. Before he left England, he preached a sermon about his idea. The colony should be built on love and kindness. They would be an example to the rest of the world. They would be like a "City on a Hill," he said, with everyone watching what they did.

Winthrop governed the colony for a long time. He did his best to make his ideas really happen. Today, he would seem very strict. For a Puritan, though, he was actually not very harsh. He tried to be reasonable. He

John Winthrop

tried to make good decisions that would help the whole community.

The Puritans were different from the Pilgrims who had settled in Plymouth. The Pilgrims hadn't had a lot of money. They were ordinary people, farmers and workmen. They went to the New World because they were looking for a place they could worship as they wanted. They weren't really trying to start a new country.

The Puritans, though, were richer than the Pilgrims. A lot of them had been lawyers or businessmen in England. They believed in hard work. They also thought getting rich was a good thing.

The Puritans wanted their own country. They wanted a chance to make the laws they thought were important. They liked the ideas in John Winthrop's "City on a Hill" sermon. They had given up on fixing the things they thought were wrong with England. They were starting over. And this time they wanted to do things right.

What a person believed was very important in their new government. A person had to be a church member to serve as a government leader, for example—or even to vote. Religious leaders couldn't be government leaders, though. The Puritans had seen bad things happen back in England when religious leaders had too much power.

The problem with the Puritans' ideas was that not everyone agreed with them. So what happened when somebody didn't go along with the leaders?

Anne Hutchison was an important woman in Puritan New England. She stood up to the religious leaders and told them they were wrong. She believed that God's approval couldn't be earned by working hard. She said that God loved people no matter what. The Massachusetts Bay Colony's leader threw her out. She and her leaders went to what would become Rhode Island and started a new colony there.

IS AMERICA BETTER?

The idea that America was different—and better—than other countries started with the Puritans. That idea would continue to grow as the country grew. Sometimes the idea would help America—and sometimes it would hurt it. What do you think about this idea? Is America really better than other countries? In what ways might it be true? Are there any ways it isn't true? Why might it be good for a country to think it's better than other countries? Why might it be bad for a country to believe that?

Punishments in the Massachusetts Bay Colony could be harsh. Somebody who didn't agree with the church or the government leaders could lose all his belongings, be kicked out of town—or even be killed.

The Puritans believed in keeping their religion "pure." If someone started talking about ideas the leaders didn't like, that person had to leave.

Of course, some people did not agree with everything the church leaders taught. These people sometimes moved away and started new colonies, away from Massachusetts Bay. So the American colonies kept spreading and growing.

Roger Williams' arrival in Rhode Island

Chapter Three
RHODE ISLAND AND CONNECTICUT

Roger Williams arrived in the Massachusetts Bay Colony in 1631. He was a young pastor with strong ideas.

When Williams and his young wife first arrived in Boston, everyone was happy to see them. Williams was likable and popular.

But then the pastor of the church went back to England and asked Williams to fill in for him. Williams said no. He thought the Massachusetts Bay Colony should never have promised **allegiance** to the king of England. He wasn't interested in being part of a church he thought was on the wrong track.

The people were offended, but a lot of people still liked Williams. Soon, the settlers in Salem invited him to be their pastor. This time, he said yes. He thought the church in Salem was better than the one in Boston. Here, he thought, he could make a difference.

But problems came up again. Williams made people uncomfortable. He told them the land really belonged to the Native people. He also didn't think people should have to pay taxes to the church. He didn't think laws should tell people they had to go to church,

When someone gives their **allegiance** to someone, it means he will serve and obey that person.

25

Roger Williams and Native Americans

either. The Puritans had come to the New World to get away from the church trying to tell them what to do. Now, Williams believed, the Puritans were acting in exactly the same way.

The leaders of the Massachusetts Bay Colony didn't like Roger Williams' ideas. They didn't like how he criticized them and stirred up trouble. But they didn't know how to get rid of him.

Finally, the colony leaders had their chance. Salem and Massachusetts Bay both wanted the same piece of land. The courts had to decide who would get the land. They saw how they could get rid of Roger Williams.

"You can have the land," the court told the people of Salem, "but only if you fire Williams as your pastor."

Salem tried to argue at first, but the court kept pushing. Finally, they agreed to get rid of Williams. They were going to send him back to England. When Williams heard what had happened, though, he left town. He went to live with a Native tribe for the winter.

In the spring of 1636, Williams' family and his friends from Salem traveled south from Massachusetts Bay. There they began a new colony—Rhode

Providence, Rhode Island

Island. Williams bought a piece of land from the Native people there, and the group built the city of Providence.

From the start, Rhode Island was different. People could disagree with each other about their religion and still work together. The first Pilgrims had come to the New World looking for freedom to worship God as they believed. Roger Williams wanted this freedom to be for everybody, not just for Puritans.

Around the same time that Roger Williams was **founding** Rhode Island, Thomas Hooker was founding the colony of Connecticut. Like Williams, Hooker had problems with the way the Massachusetts Bay Colony governed. Hooker was not really upset about wanting more religious freedom, though. He was bothered that only men who owned land and were church members could vote. He thought all men should be able to vote, whether or not they owned land. (Nobody even thought about women voting at this time.)

When Thomas Hooker moved away from Massachusetts Bay and built Connecticut, he was trying to make a community that would let all men take part in government. He believed

Statue of Thomas Hooker

Founding a new place means starting it or setting it up for settlers.

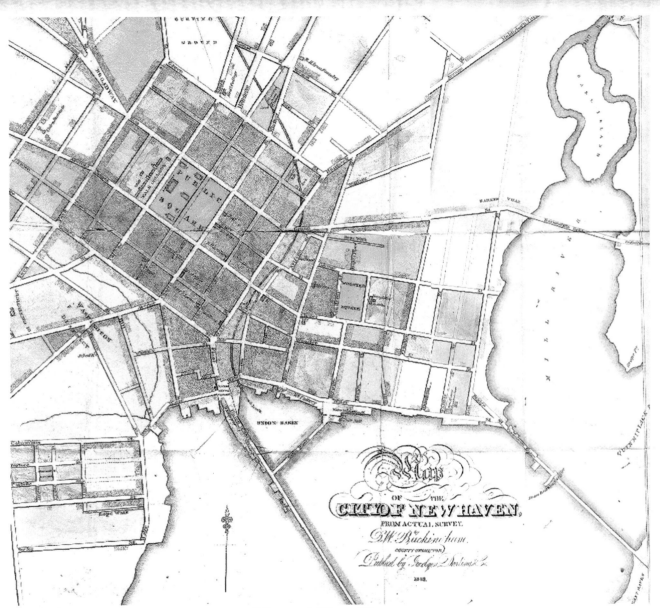

Map of New Haven

this was a right and freedom that God meant for people to have.

In April 1638, another group arrived in Connecticut. This group was led by Reverend John Davenport. They had gone first to Massachusetts Bay, but they hadn't liked it there. They thought the people of Massachusetts Bay weren't as strict in their religion as they should be.

When Reverend Davenport and the five hundred people with him got to Connecticut, they started building the town of New Haven. They had big plans for New Haven. It was going to be the perfect Christian town. The laws and government would be based on Puritan beliefs. Also, they wanted New Haven to be a trading center. They wanted to make money selling and trading furs and fish.

F. Halpin. sc

Reverend John Davenport

New Haven wasn't able to make lots of money the way they had hoped, though. They filled up a ship with their goods, to take back to England. But the ship was lost at sea.

An **independent** community doesn't need anyone else for support or to tell it how to behave.

RELIGION AND THE GOVERNMENT

Williams thought the church should focus on helping people follow God. Making laws and running the colony shouldn't be the church's job. Hundreds of years later, people in the United States would still be arguing about how much control churches should have. For instance, today people wonder if the Bible should be allowed to be quoted in public places. Should religious holidays be celebrated in school? What do you think?

Although New Haven was in Connecticut, it was an **independent** community that governed itself. Eventually, in 1664, New Haven joined the rest of the towns in Connecticut. Getting rich on its own hadn't worked out for the colony. So now it gave up its independence.

Chapter Four
NEW NETHERLAND AND NEW SWEDEN

The colony of New Netherland was formed because the Dutch were looking for the Northwest Passage.

The Northwest Passage was an idea—the idea that maybe, just maybe there was a quick and easy route from the Atlantic Ocean to the Pacific. At the time, people who wanted to travel to Asia either had to travel by land—a long, hard, and expensive trip—or else they had to sail around the bottom of Africa or South America. Sailing so far south took a long time. The voyages were dangerous, too. Lots of ships sank. Trading companies lost lots of money when so much of their goods were destroyed.

In 1608, a Dutch trading company hired the English explorer Henry Hudson to find the Northwest Passage. They told Hudson to sail north, through the Arctic Ocean. Instead, he sailed west. Hudson knew what he was doing. He had sailed north before. He knew the way was blocked by ice. He was pretty sure the Arctic Ocean wasn't the Northwest Passage everyone was looking for.

Along the coast of the New World, through what is now New York Harbor, Hudson discovered a wide river. (Later, the river would be named after him—the Hudson River.) He sailed upriver. He hoped it would take him all the way through North America to

HALF MOON

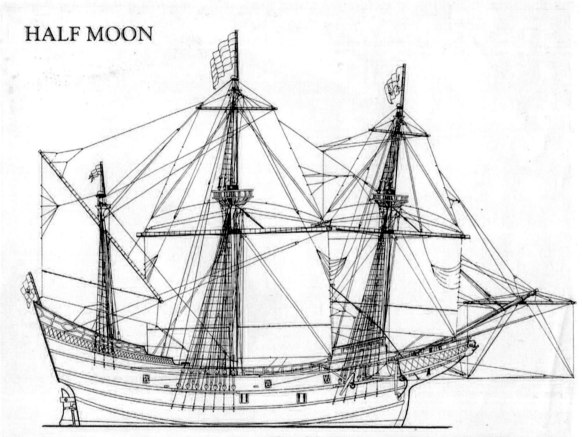

The Half Moon, Henry Hudson's ship

the Pacific Ocean. Instead, 150 miles on his way, his ship ran aground. The river was too shallow for him to go any further. So he turned around and went back to Europe.

The Dutch who had hired Hudson were upset with him. He hadn't gone north like they'd told him to. They wondered if he really wanted them to find the Northwest Passage at all. Maybe, they thought, he was secretly working for the English.

Still, Hudson had found some interesting things. The Dutch sent more ships back to look around some more. The area looked good for furs and trade. They decided to start a new colony there.

The Dutch claimed the Hudson River and the land around it. They called the colony New Netherland. Then they built Fort Orange, a trading post, at the point in the river where Hudson had run aground. (The modern city of Albany, New York, is in the same place where Fort Orange once was.)

The Dutch wanted New Netherland to make lots of money for them. But running a colony cost too much. They had to build forts. They had to pay soldiers and doctors and other people to work at the forts. So the Dutch gave away pieces of land in New Netherland. The new landowners agreed to pay for a certain number of people to settle on their land. In return, the Dutch kept all the fur trading rights for the colony.

This system worked for a while. Some men made a lot of money and built towns on their land. Then, in 1647, Peter Stuyvesant became the new director of the Dutch West India Company.

Henry Hudson

Stuyvesant moved to New Amsterdam (which would be renamed New York City twenty years later). Right away, he started making changes. He raised taxes and made new laws that upset a lot of people. The landowners didn't like Stuyvesant trying to take away their power.

The trouble between Stuyvesant and the landowners went on for a long time. When the landowners complained, the trading company tried to get Stuyvesant to go back to the Netherlands. He refused to go.

Then, in 1664, the English attacked New Amsterdam. The English owned almost all the rest of the East Coast of North America. Now they thought they should own New Netherland, too.

At first, Stuyvesant tried to fight the English. The people of New Amsterdam wanted to surrender. They didn't want to fight. They didn't want people to get killed. Finally, Stuyvesant agreed to give up.

The Dutch government didn't want to lose its North American colony, though. For two years, the Dutch fought against the English in Europe. In 1667, the Netherlands signed a treaty with England, ending the war. England got to keep New Netherland, which they called New York. The Netherlands got to keep another colony that was in South America.

Back in 1626, when the Dutch had first built New Amsterdam, the first governor had been Peter Minuit. Minuit had lost his job after trouble with the landowners. When Minuit heard that Sweden was thinking about starting its own colony, he asked for the job.

In the 1600s, Sweden was a large and powerful country—much larger and more powerful that it is today. Sweden owned a lot of land in Europe, but it didn't have a colony in North America.

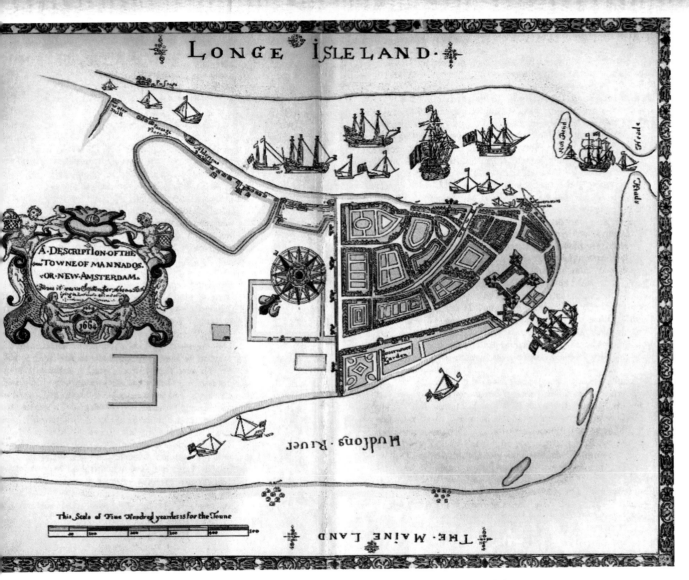

Map of New Amsterdam (Manhattan), 1664

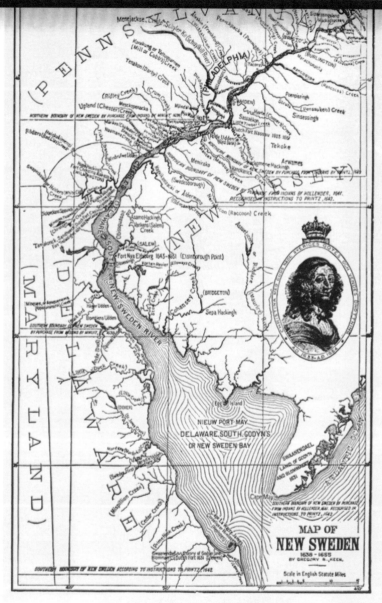

Map of New Sweden

In 1638, Peter Minuit arrived in the New World with two ships of settlers. They built a fort at what is today Wilmington, Delaware. They named it Fort Christina, after Sweden's twelve-year-old queen.

New Sweden had trouble finding people who wanted to move to their colony, though. People in Sweden weren't having religious problems, like the Puritans had. They didn't seem likely to get rich in the little colony, either. So New Sweden found married soldiers who had gotten into trouble with the law. They offered the soldiers a choice. They could either go to prison for their crimes in Sweden or they could move to New Sweden. In New Sweden, they would be able to make a new life for themselves and their families.

Once they had built New Sweden, though, the New Sweden

Peter Stuyvesant

trading company didn't spend a lot of time thinking about its colony. The governor of the colony, Johan Printz, didn't like his job, either. The company told him to keep doing his job, because they didn't have anyone to replace him.

In 1651, the Dutch, led by Peter Stuyvesant, attacked New Sweden and claimed it. The New Sweden Company didn't answer when Printz asked for help. New Sweden left the northern part of their colony to the Dutch and stayed mostly around Fort Christina.

By 1653, the Swedish colonists were miserable. The weather had been terrible, which meant their crops hadn't grown well. They didn't have a lot of food. They were worried about the Dutch. Printz had gotten sick and wasn't much help either.

Frustrated, Printz went back to Sweden to talk to the company's leaders face-to-face. The New Sweden Company sent Johan Rising to replace him.

Rising did what he could. He tried to drive the Dutch out of New Sweden. Instead, he just made them mad. After Rising had captured one of the Dutch forts, Stuyvesant came back and took over all of New Sweden.

The Dutch let the Swedish people stay in the area and set up their own government. Then, when the English took over New Netherland, they gained control over New Sweden as well.

Chapter Five
PENNSYLVANIA AND NEW JERSEY

Even though it had been settled for less than fifty years, by the 1670s, New Jersey had already belonged to several different groups. The southern part had been first settled by New Sweden. The Dutch had claimed most of the coastline. Then, when the English took over New Netherland and New Sweden, the area was renamed New Jersey.

In 1673, William Penn and eleven other **Quakers** were able to buy the western part of New Jersey. Then Penn convinced King Charles II to give him a large piece of land further west from New Jersey. King Charles had owed Penn's father money, and the land paid the debt. Penn named the area Pennsylvania—which meant Penn's Woods. He had big plans for the new colony.

William Penn had been raised in the Anglican Church in England. Ever since he was a teenager, though, he'd been getting into trouble because of his religious ideas. He was

Quakers belong to a Christian group that began in the 1600s. They believe in living simply and working for peace.

William Penn as a young man.

very interested in the things the Quakers taught, and the Anglican Church didn't approve of the Quakers.

The Quakers believed that people were naturally good. They thought that God could talk to people who had never even read the Bible. They didn't believe in making people go to church. They also didn't believe in church buildings or ministers. They believed that any building could be a church and any person could be a minister. They thought God cared more about your attitudes and how you acted than about how you worshipped Him.

When Penn was twenty-three years old, he decided to become a Quaker. Being a Quaker was against the law in England, but Penn didn't care. He thought being a Quaker was the right thing to do. So that's what he did.

By the time he helped start the first Quaker colony in the western part of New Jersey, Penn had already spent time in jail for his beliefs. He was determined that the new colony would be a place where people wouldn't be punished for the things they believed. He wanted Pennsylvania to be a "holy experiment." The colony wouldn't make any laws about religion. People could worship as they wanted.

The laws in Pennsylvania were not strict. Because Quakers thought people were basically

THE
FRAME
OF THE
Government of Pennsilvania
IN
AMERICA, &c.

To all People, to whom these Presents shall come:

WHEREAS King Charles the Second, by his Letters Patents, under the Great Seal of England, for the Considerations therein mentioned, hath been graciously pleased to Give and Grant unto Me William Penn (by the Name of William Penn Esquire, Son and Heir of Sir William Penn deceased) and to My Heirs and Assigns forever, All that Tract of Land or Province, called Pennsilvania, in America, with divers great Powers, Preheminencies, Royalties, Jurisdictions and Authorities necessary for the Well-being and Government thereof

Now know Ye, That for the Well-being and Government of the said Province, and for the Encouragement of all the Free-men and Planters that may be therein concerned, in pursuance of the Powers aforementioned, I the said William Penn have Declared, Granted and Confirmed, and by these Presents for Me, my Heirs and Assigns do Declare, Grant and Confirm unto all the Free-men, Planters and Adventurers of, in and to the said Province These Liberties, Franchises and Properties to be held, enjoyed and kept by the Free-men, Planters and Inhabitants of and in the said Province of Pennsilvania forever.

Imprimis, That the Government of this Province shall, according to the Powers of the Patent, consist of the Governour and Free-men of the said Province, in the Form of a Provincial Council and General Assembly, by whom all Laws shall be made, Officers chosen and publick Affairs Transacted, as is hereafter respectively declared; That is to say,

II. That the Free-men of the said Province shall on the Twentieth day of the Twelfth Moneth, which shall be in this present Year One Thousand Six Hundred Eighty and Two, Meet and Assembly in some fit place, of which timely Notice shall be beforehand given by the Governour or his Deputy, and then and there shall chuse out of themselves Seventy Two Persons of most Note for their Wisdom, Virtue and Ability, who shall meet on the Tenth day of the First Moneth next ensuing, and alwayes be called and act as the Provincial Council of the said Province.

First page of Penn's "Frame of Government"

good, they didn't believe people needed a lot of laws. They thought people would usually do the right thing.

Penn wrote a booklet about his new colony to make people want to come live there. The booklet told about how all children could get an education. It described the religious freedoms and easy laws. Also, the booklet told how much it cost to buy land in Pennsylvania. Penn was selling land very cheaply.

Soon, thousands of people were hurrying to move to Pennsylvania. Three thousand came the first year. By the seventh year, the population had grown to twelve thousand.

William Penn spent a lot of his time taking care of his colony. He also needed to make sure the colony paid taxes to the king in England. That was hard to do without strict laws. Penn went back and forth between America and England, trying to make sure everyone stayed happy.

Penn wasn't very good at details, though. He liked thinking about the best way things could be—but he didn't always make good decisions when things went wrong. The person who was supposed to help him take care of his money ended up cheating him and stealing from him. Penn loaned people money but didn't do anything when they didn't pay him back. His son ran up big debts. Eventually, Penn ran out of money.

The dream Penn had for Pennsylvania didn't work out exactly as he had hoped. People didn't do the right thing as much as Penn thought they

William Penn

would. After he died, in 1718, the colony stopped focusing on religious freedom quite as much. Pennsylvania kept a lot of William Penn's ideas, though.

Fifty years later, the new country of the United States would be born in the city of Philadelphia. Penn's ideas about people having equal rights would be very important to that new country. His ideas about different kinds of people living together would be important as well.

The new country would become known as a place where people from all over the world could come and live. No matter what a person's religion was, or what a person's beliefs were, or how a person lived, everyone would be accepted.

Even though things didn't always work out that way—either in William Penn's time or in our own—that is still the idea on which the United States is built.

WHAT DO YOU THINK?

What things would William Penn like about the United States today? What things wouldn't he like?

FIND OUT MORE

In Books

Bjornlund, Lydia. *Massachusetts*. San Diego, Calif.: Lucent Books, 2002.

Kline, Andrew A. *Rhode Island*. San Diego, Calif.: Lucent Books, 2002.

Lukes, Bonnie L. *Colonial America*. San Diego, Calif.: Lucent Books, 2000.

Sherrow, Victoria. *Pennsylvania*. San Diego, Calif.: Lucent Books, 2002.

Streissguth, Thomas. *New Jersey*. San Diego, Calif.: Lucent Books, 2002.

On the Internet

Pilgrims and Massachusetts Bay Colony
www.usahistory.info/New-England

Rhode Island
www.rogerwilliams.org/biography.htm

Connecticut
www.colonialwarsct.org/index.htm

New Netherland
www.newnetherland.org

New Sweden
www.colonialswedes.org

Pennsylvania
www.legis.state.pa.us/WU01/VC/visitor_info/pa_history/pa_history.htm

INDEX

ABOUT THE AUTHOR
AND THE CONSULTANT

Teresa LaClair is an author who lives in New York State, but she was born in Canada. She has also written other books for kids.

Dr. Jack N. Rakove is a professor of history and American studies at Stanford University, where he is director of American studies. The winner of the 1997 Pulitzer Prize in history, Dr. Rakove is the author of *The Unfinished Election of 2000, Constitutional Culture and Democratic Rule*, and *James Madison and the Creation of the American Republic*. He is also the president of the Society for the History of the Early American Republic.